The Case of the Missing Math Teacher

written by Suzanne Weyn
illustrated by K. Michael Crawford

McGraw-Hill School Division
New York Farmington

"Okay, settle down now, class. Class, come on, listen up! Class, please—I'd like your attention up here in the front of the room!" Ms. Rhombus realized defeat and her face reddened even more.

It wasn't any use. The class continued to ignore her. They talked, threw spitballs, and passed notes. It was as if their math teacher wasn't even in the building, let alone in front of the room.

"Pay attention, class—this is your final warning!" Ms. Rhombus cried above the noise level.

"Poor, Ms. Rhombus," thought Rae Gonzalez again, "this really isn't right. She's only trying to teach us mathematics."

Rae glanced around the classroom. Not all of the students were being terrible—she counted several who were just sitting there looking bored and disgusted, like Nicholas Karras, the class brain.

Ms. Rhombus had finished writing and was now collecting her books and her purse. She addressed the class again in a loud voice, saying, "You kids must certainly know your math. Obviously you're totally satisfied with your knowledge of the subject, so there's no reason for my being here, now is there? That being the case, I'm leaving. If you have second thoughts and you decide you'd like to learn something, you'll just have to come find me."

With that, Ms. Rhombus pushed in her chair and walked out the door. The class just sat there blinking for a moment—everyone was stunned. Now that you could hear a pin drop, everyone half-expected her to come back in—but no, minutes passed and still no Ms. Rhombus.

"Do you think she went to get Principal Milton?" Sean McDougal asked. The moment he said that, the whole class faced forward and folded their hands.

Several more minutes passed, and Ms. Rhombus still hadn't returned—with or without the principal.

“Well, where could she be?” Emily Ywahoo cried.

“Maybe she’ll never come back and we’ll never have to do math again,” Parker Perry spoke up.

Some kids cheered and jumped out of their seats, dancing an impromptu conga around the back table, while others still looked worried.

Then Rae stood up and shouted, “We shouldn’t be having a celebration. We hurt Ms. Rhombus’s feelings and I want to go find her. Who wants to come with me?”

Emily was the first to walk to the door. Then Sean did the same, followed by Dilip Patel.

"Is that all?" Rae asked the class, as she walked over to the other three.

That's when Allyson Chen followed Rae to the door. "Nobody else wants to look for Ms. Rhombus?" Rae asked for the last time, but everyone else stayed put.

Some kids went back to being wild. Others, like Nicholas, continued to sit like angels, in case the principal walked in.

As the five kids stepped out into the hall, Dilip shifted awkwardly from one foot to the other. “Do you think we’ll get in trouble for leaving class?” he asked nervously. “Maybe we need to be officially released first?”

“I don’t know,” Rae admitted. Then, spotting a card taped to the wall and pulling it down, she cried, “Look! It may be some kind of clue!”

Emily took the card from her and read:

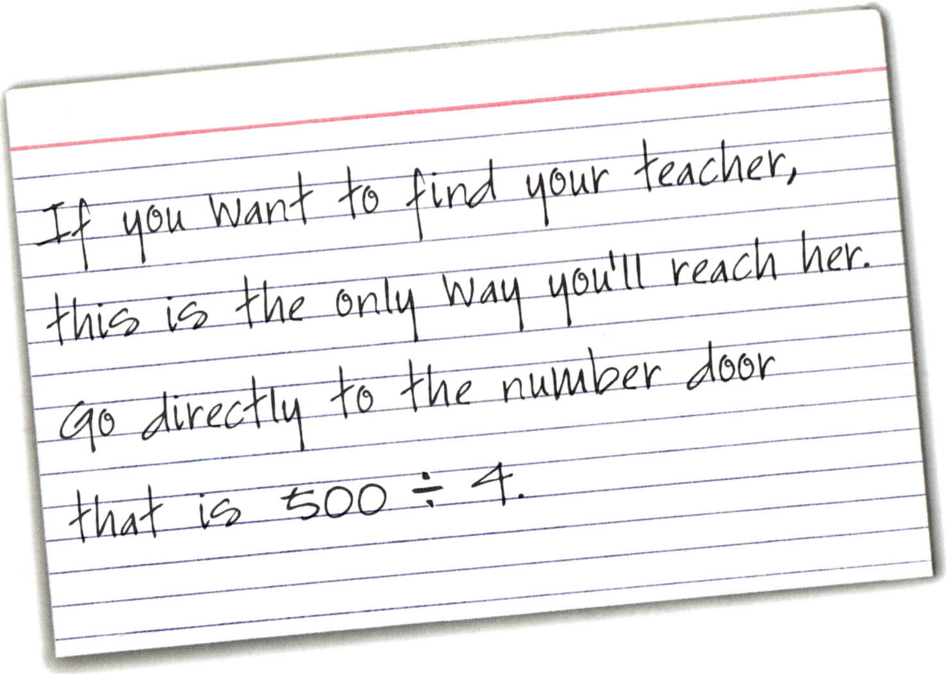

The kids looked at one another. Then Sean cried, "It's a riddle! Let's do the math to solve it!"

Emily took a pad and pencil from her backpack and worked it out in long division. Meanwhile, Sean divided 500 in half and then in half one more time. "One hundred and twenty-five!" Emily and Sean shouted together.

"That's the science room!" Rae cried excitedly. "Come on!" she called over her shoulder as she walked as quickly as she could down the hall, the others following in tow.

When they got to the science room, no one was there. The light had been turned off, and the door was closed. Dilip tried the knob anyway—and found the door was unlocked!

H_2O =
CO =

After putting on the light and going in, Ms. Rhombus's loyal students fanned out and began searching for clues. Rae even picked up a magnifying glass in case they found something that required careful inspection.

As he turned the corner of a work station, Dilip knocked over a glass bottle and a little pile of dried red and yellow flakes fell out. "What is this spice doing here?" he wondered aloud. Rae bent down to examine the spill, murmuring, "Maybe it's a clue!"

"Or maybe Mr. Feudi just brought in pizza again for lunch," Allyson guessed. Then, spotting something sticking out from underneath the counter, she added, "Hey, but this may be what we're looking for," as she pulled down the card that had been taped there.

Allyson read the clue aloud:

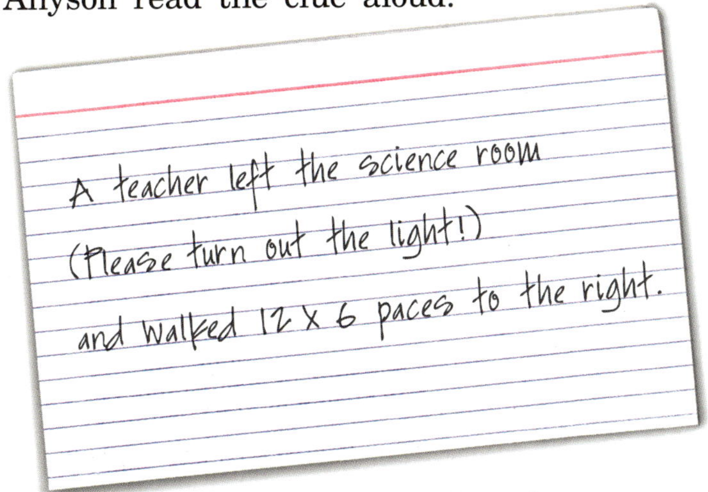
A teacher left the science room
(Please turn out the light!)
and walked 12 x 6 paces to the right.

Dilip went to the blackboard to figure out the math. “Seventy-two paces to the right,” he announced.

Just as Rae shut off the light, Nicholas Karras and two other kids joined them in the hall. Sean filled them in as the others counted out the paces.

Rae took the next clue off the Music Room door and read: “Turn left and walk 13 x 6 paces
Down the other hall. Happy faces!”

Nicholas, who had gotten out his calculator to figure it out, announced, “Seventy-eight paces to the left.”

Taped to the back wall of the cafeteria, right by a kettle of lentil and onion soup, the kids found the next card. Dilip read it for the others:

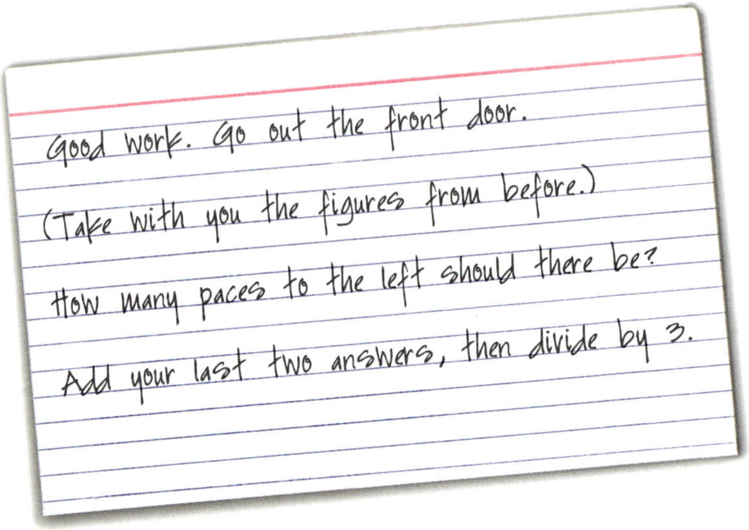

"That's seventy-two plus seventy-eight, which is one hundred and fifty," Nicholas declared, after tapping on the keys of his calculator.

"Divided by three, that makes fifty!" Emily cried.

Together, they walked fifty steps across the playground and entered the side door of the gym.

"Oh, my gosh!" Rae gasped.

"Sorry to disturb you," Dilip exclaimed, because Ms. Rhombus was facing the bleachers, addressing a group of eight men and women the children had never seen before.

"No, it's all right—please come on in, kids! You found me!" Ms. Rhombus cried happily. "You found me—but, I must say, I'm disappointed that there aren't more of you?"

Ms. Rhombus's students shrugged. "We really want you to come back, though," Emily said.

Then Sean stepped forward and said, "Excuse me, Ms. Rhombus, but what are you doing here, anyway? You left us clues by the math class, the science room, the music room, and the cafeteria. Then we find you here in the gym—I don't get it," he admitted, looking puzzled.

Ms. Rhombus smiled and replied in a gentle voice, "What do mathematicians, scientists, musicians, cooks, cashiers, and athletes all have in common?"

"They all use math!" the students cried.

Then Ms. Rhombus introduced the kids to the people she had been speaking with. The first man built scale models of buildings for architects; then there were two women—one was a research scientist and the other was a composer. The fourth person was a chef, and then the last four people were a salesperson, a medical attendant from the hospital, a baseball player, and a ballet dancer.

The students were all excited to hear what the school's guests did for a living, but their faces clearly showed that they didn't yet understand what any of that had to do with them.

"We're putting together a Math Career Day here at school," Ms. Rhombus explained, adding, "this way students will get an opportunity to see just how often math is used in careers every day."

"What a great idea!" exclaimed Dilip.

"And because you came to find me, I have a special surprise for you!" added Ms. Rhombus.

"What kind of surprise?" asked Emily excitedly.

"These wonderful people have agreed to work with you for the next two weeks until our career day," replied Ms. Rhombus. "They will answer your questions and even help you with a project by e-mail!"

"What about the remainder of the class?" Dilip asked.

"Well, Mr. Milton is with them by now," Ms. Rhombus responded vaguely.

"Then it's curtains for them!" blurted Rae.

"Not exactly," said Ms. Rhombus with a smile, "but they certainly won't be able to work one-on-one with a mentor. It's a shame that more students didn't care enough about their studies to go with you."

Ms. Rhombus asked the kids to choose a mentor. "Don't quarrel over them now! They all have so much to share about how mathematics helps them every day in their careers."

Rae and her friends were really glad they had gone to look for Ms. Rhombus and solved all the math riddles in her teacher hunt. They all felt they had won a fabulous prize—and a valuable opportunity.

Peering through her magnifying glass, Rae whispered to Allyson, "One thing's for certain, the case of the missing math teacher is definitely closed."